ja   **Bush Theatre**

MAGGOTS
by Farah Najib

Maggots was first performed in this version
at the Bush Theatre, London, on 27 January 2026,
produced by Jessie Anand Productions
in association with the Bush Theatre.

MAGGOTS
by Farah Najib

Cast

Sam Baker Jones
Safiyya Ingar
Marcia Lecky

Creative Team

Writer	Farah Najib
Director	Jess Barton
Set & Costume Designer	Caitlin Mawhinney
Lighting Designer	Peter Small
Composer & Sound Designer	Duramaney Kamara
Casting Director	Fran Cattaneo
Producer	Jessie Anand
Production Manager	Adam Jefferys
Stage Manager	Rose Hockaday

For Bush Theatre

Producer	Emma Halstead
Bush Dramaturg	Olivia Poglio-Nwabali
Original Dramaturg	Titilola Dawudu
Press Manager	Martin Shippen
Marketing Campaign Lead	Amelia White
Technical & Buildings Manager	Jamie Haigh

CAST

Sam Baker Jones

Sam Baker Jones most recently wrapped *Dear England* for the BBC, in the role of Jack Grealish, and *Trigger Point* for ITV. He can be seen in a leading role in *Murder Before Evensong* opposite Amit Shah. Sam's other screen credits include *The Walk In* (opposite Stephen Graham) and *Noughts + Crosses* (BBC). Stage work includes *Big Big Sky* (New Vic); *Here* (Southwark Playhouse); *Swim, Aunty, Swim!* (Belgrade).

Marcia Lecky

Marcia Lecky trained at the American Academy of Dramatic Art in New York and at Guildford School of Acting.

Her theatre includes: *Anna Karenina* (Chichester); *Coriolanus, The House of Bernarda Alba, Much Ado About Nothing, The Curious Incident of the Dog in the Night-Time, Paradise, Top Girls* (National); *Cymbeline* (RSC); *The Scottsboro Boys* (Garrick); *The Launderette* (Anima Theatre Company at VAULT).

Marcia's television appearances include: *Brian and Maggie, EastEnders, Emmerdale, Grace, Wreck, Ten Percent, Ted Lasso, Hollyoaks, Holby City, Not Going Out, Doctors, Doctor Who, Casualty,* and *Dawn*. Films include: *Breaking Infinity* and *Kingslayer*. Marcia is also a voice-over artist and has worked on various BBC projects.

Safiyya Ingar

Safiyya Ingar is an actor and VO artist from London. After graduating from their alma mater in 2017, they have nurtured their career and skills in theatre, TV, film, and voice acting.

Theatre includes: *King Troll* (New Diorama); *Two Billion Beats* (Orange Tree); *The Box of Delights* (Wilton's Music Hall); *Marvin's Binoculars, The Canterville Ghost* (Unicorn); *Hobson's Choice* (Royal Exchange); *Holes, LAVA* (Nottingham Playhouse); *Growth* (Paines Plough/UK tour).

Screen credits include: *Brides* (BFI/Neon Films) for which they were nominated for 2 BIFA Awards; *The Witcher* – Series 3 & 4 (Netflix); and *Layla* (BFI/Film4).

Video games: *Diablo IV* (Blizzard), *Valkyrie Elysium* (Square Enix), *Dustborn* (Quantic Dream/Red Thread Games), *Wuthering Waves* (Kuro Games).

They are also known for their work as the original companion, Valarie Lockwood, in Big Finish's award-winning audio series *Doctor Who: The Eleventh Doctor Chronicles*.

CREATIVE TEAM

Farah Najib | Writer

Farah Najib is an award-winning playwright and alumna of the Royal Court Writers' Group and Soho Theatre Writers' Lab. Her play *Dirty Dogs* won the 2020 Tony Craze Award from Soho Theatre and was longlisted for the 2022 Bruntwood Prize for Playwriting. She trained in Writing for Performance at the Royal Central School of Speech & Drama.

Jess Barton | Director

Jess Barton is a director and theatre maker based in East London. She specialises in new writing, primarily that which interrogates what it means to be human.

Credits include: *Maggots, Don't Forget My Face, AAAAA* (co-director with David Brady), *Feel More, At Last* (co-director with David Brady), *Like You Hate Me* (Lion and Unicorn); *Diversifications* (Old Red Lion); *Refuge, Mnemonic* (The Space); *Lemons Lemons Lemons Lemons Lemons* (Tour); *The Last Five Years, Company* (Marlborough); *RENT* (Sallis Benney).

Caitlin Mawhinney | Set & Costume Designer

Caitlin Mawhinney is a set and costume designer whose work has been seen on stages and unconventional spaces across the country. Caitlin was the winner of the Evening Standard Future Theatre Fund in Visual Design and has continued to gain recognition with nominations for The Stage Debut Awards; the Arts Foundation Futures Award; The Naomi Wilkinson Award For Stage Design; and finalist for the JMK Awards.

Recent collaborations include National Theatre, Hull Truck Theatre, Leeds Playhouse, The Pleasance, Soho Theatre, Arcola Theatre, Theatre503, Chichester Festival Theatre, Northern Opera and Southbank Centre, alongside many others.

Peter Small | Lighting Designer

Peter is an Offie and Theatre & Technology Award nominated lighting designer working across mediums such as theatre, dance, opera and immersive. As well as his work on stage, Peter designed the lighting for the Garden Cinema in Covent Garden, and was a judge for the inaugural Profile Awards.

Credits include: *Kathy and Stella Solve a Murder!* (Ambassadors/Bristol Old Vic/HOME Manchester/Edinburgh); *ROAM* (Shaftesbury Theatre); *King Stakh's Wild Hunt* (Barbican); *Baby Reindeer* (Bush/Edinburgh); *All or Nothing* (West End/UK Tour); *What Remains of Us* (Bristol Old Vic); *KS6: Small Forward* (Barbican/La MaMa); *Spitfire Girls* (UK Tour); *The School for Scandal* (UK Tour); *Lady Chatterley's Lover* (UK Tour); *Orlando* (59E59); *Wahnfried:*

The Birth of the Wagner Cult, Il barbiere di Siviglia, Pelléas et Mélisande, Dido and Aeneas (Longborough Festival Opera); *Shrek the Musical* and *My Fair Lady* (Mercury Theatre); *Cinderella* (Queen's Theatre Hornchurch); *The Misandrist* (Arcola); *Sylvia* and *Nunsense* (English Theatre Frankfurt); *Twelfth Night* (Kew Gardens); *RED* (Polka); *LIT* (Nottingham Playhouse); *58th Street, The Great Murder Mystery, The Greatest Night of the Jazz Age* and *The Great Christmas Feast* (The Lost Estate); *The Ritual Slaughter of Gorge Mastromas, The Caucasian Chalk Circle, The Priory* and *A Skull in Connemara* (Dailes Theatre); *17 Minutes* (Edinburgh); *Square Go* (UK Tour/59E59/Edinburgh). Peter studied at the Royal Academy of Dramatic Art and now lights productions across theatre, dance and opera.

He was nominated for two 2018 Off West End Best Lighting Awards for *Black Mountain* (Orange Tree) and *A Girl In School Uniform (Walks Into a Bar)* (New Diorama), for which he was also a finalist for the 2018 Theatre & Technology Award for Creative Innovation in Lighting. His lighting design for *58th Street* was nominated for the ABTT Stephen Joseph Award.

Duramaney Kamara | Composer & Sound Designer

Duramaney Kamara is a multidisciplinary sound designer and composer. Under the pseudonym 'D L K', he is also a recording artist and producer who releases music under his indie label BE FREE 888 REPERTOIRE.

Theatre credits include: *Going Out Out* (HOME); *Bangers* (Arcola/Soho/Edinburgh Fringe); *Wolves On Road, August in England, House of Ife, Project 2036* (Bush); *Barcelona* (West End); *Grow Up, C3 Stories* (Company Three); *MANTELPEACE* (Young Vic Taking Part); *Swim, Aunty, Swim!* (Belgrade); *Love Steps* (Omnibus/Wrested Veil); *Cinderella* (Brixton House); *Clyde's* (Donmar); *Sucker Punch* (Queen's, Hornchurch); *Bootycandy* (Gate); *Anansi the Spider* (Unicorn/Regent's Park Open Air); *Christmas in the Sunshine* (Unicorn); *Moreno, Roman Candle* (Theatre503); *Collection* (Tara Arts); *The Death of a Black Man, Hoes* (Hampstead); *The Dark* (Fuel/Ovalhouse); *Living Newspaper Edition 4 & 5, Dismantle This Room, My Mum's a Twat, Instructions for Correct Assembly, katzenmusik* (Royal Court).

Fran Cattaneo | Casting Director

Fran Cattaneo is a casting director based in London, where she has assisted in the offices of Rory Okey, Dan Hubbard and Heather Basten for screen and, for stage, Harry Blumenau, Lotte Hines at the Donmar Warehouse and Stuart Burt.

Her credits for theatre include acting as Casting Director on *FXFest Readings* (Soho); *Selina Thompson's Twine* (Yard); *The Bleeding Tree* directed by The Stage Debut Award-winning director Sophie Drake (Southwark); *The Great Privation: How to Flip Ten Cents into a Dollar* (Theatre503); consulting on *This Might Not Be It*, *...blackbird hour* (Bush).

Adam Jefferys | Production Manager

Adam is an award nominated lighting designer and production manager from Essex. Recent work includes: *Jack and the Beanstalk* (Queen's Theatre Hornchurch); *A Shoddy Christmas Carol* (Lichfield Garrick); *Three Little Pigs* (Unicorn/Chichester); *Speed* (Bush); *Animal Farm* (Bolton Octagon and UK Tour); *Statues* (Bush); *Foreverland* (Southwark Playhouse); *Playfight* (Summerhall/Edinburgh); *Communion* (Bush); *The End* (Bush); *My Father's Fable* (Bush); *The Bleeding Tree* (Southwark Playhouse); *Murder in the Dark* (UK Tour); *Elephant* (Bush); *After the Act* (New Diorama); *War & Culture* (New Diorama); *Under the Kundè Tree* (Southwark Playhouse); *Jekyll and Hyde* (Derby Theatre); *Project Dictator* (New Diorama/Edinburgh); *Everything Has Changed* (UK Tour/Edinburgh); *Dorian* (Reading Rep).

Adam was nominated for The Stage Debut Awards 2025 for Best Designer.

Rose Hockaday | Stage Manager

Rose Hockaday (she/her) is a freelance stage manager based in London.

Theatre: *Sh!t Theatre: EVITA TOO* (Southbank Centre); *I Dream of Theresa May* (Tara Theatre); *My English Persian Kitchen* (UK/Ireland Tour); *Sh!t Theatre: Or What's Left Of Us*, *LORENZO* (2023 Fringe First winners); *Jali*, *Age Is A Feeling* (2022 Fringe First winner and 2023 Olivier Award nominee); *Bedu* (Soho); *Autumn* (Park Theatre); *Surrender* (Arcola); *Worth* (New Earth); *harmony. 天人合一*, *At Broken Bridge* and *No Particular Order* (Ellandar); *The Ex-Boyfriend Yard Sale* (London/Toronto); *A Woman Walks Into A Bank*, *Milk & Gall*, *Spiderfly*, *Wolfie* & *Art of Gaman* (Theatre503); *Antigone*, *Pops*, *You Only Live Forever* and *In Tents and Purposes* (Viscera Theatre); *Timmy*, *Glitter Punch*, *How To Survive A Post-Truth Apocalypse*, *They Built It. No One Came*, *Jericho Creek* (Fledgling Theatre).

Film: *Heaven Knows*, *Visitors*, *Ignite*, *Pomegranate*, *Wandering Eyes* and *Versions of Us*, as well as music videos *Phase Me Out*, *When You're Gone* and *Saint* for artist VÉRITÉ.

Jessie Anand | Producer

Jessie Anand is a theatre and opera producer who previously produced hit Bush Studio shows *Tender* and *This Might Not Be It*.

Other credits include: Untapped Award-winning show *The Mosinee Project* (Underbelly, Edinburgh Fringe/New Diorama); Offie Award-winning productions *The Bleeding Tree*, *Yellowfin* (Southwark); *Bungalow* (Theatre503); *Orlando* (VAULT Festival/Pleasance, Edinburgh Fringe/59E59); *Pennyroyal* (Finborough Theatre); *Cabildo* (Arcola/Wilton's Music Hall).

She works as an in-house producer at Jermyn Street Theatre and she is the company producer for Airlock Theatre, with whom she has produced shows at Soho Theatre, Edinburgh Fringe and on tour. She has also worked with and for companies including the National Theatre, Belarus Free Theatre, Wayward Productions, Kandinsky and The Big House. Jessie is supported by new producers' charity Stage One.

Bush Theatre

We make theatre for London. Now.

For over 50 years the Bush Theatre has been a world-famous home for new plays and an internationally renowned champion of playwrights.

Combining ambitious artistic programming with meaningful community engagement work and industry leading talent development schemes, the Bush Theatre champions and supports unheard voices to develop the artists and audiences of the future.

Since opening in 1972 the Bush has produced more than 500 ground-breaking premieres of new plays, developing an enviable reputation for its acclaimed productions nationally and internationally.

They have nurtured the careers of writers including James Graham, Lucy Kirkwood, Temi Wilkey, Jonathan Harvey and Jack Thorne. Recent successes include Tyrell Williams' *Red Pitch*, Benedict Lombe's *Shifters*, and Arinzé Kene's *Misty*. The Bush has won over 100 awards including the Olivier Award for Outstanding Achievement in Affliate Theatre for the past four years for Richard Gadd's *Baby Reindeer*, Igor Memic's *Old Bridge*, Waleed Akhtar's *The P Word* and Matilda Feyişayo Ibini's *Sleepova*.

Located in the renovated old library on Uxbridge Road in the heart of Shepherd's Bush, the Bush Theatre continues to create a space where all communities can be part of its future and call the theatre home.

> **'The place to go for ground-breaking work as diverse as its audiences'** EVENING STANDARD

bushtheatre.co.uk
@bushtheatre

Supported by ARTS COUNCIL ENGLAND

Artistic Director & Co-CEO	Taio Lawson
Executive Director & Co-CEO	Angela Wachner
Outgoing Artistic Director	Lynette Linton
Outgoing Executive Director	Mimi Findlay
Associate Director	Katie Greenall
Executive & Operations Assistant	Deborah Bahi
Technician	Yuval Brigg
Development Manager	Choi
Head of Development (maternity leave)	Jocelyn Cox
People & Culture Administrator	Dorothy Ekema-Walla
Finance Assistant	Lauren Francis
Head of Technical & Buildings	Jamie Haigh
Producer	Emma Halstead
Assistant Venue Manager	Rae Harm
Head of Finance	Neil Harris
Lead Producer	Nikita Karia
Box Office Supervisor	Paula Kramer
Community Producing Assistant	Joanne Leung
Event Sales Manager	Simon Pilling
Literary Manager & Lead Dramaturge	Olivia Poglio-Nwabali
Venue Manager (Theatre)	Ade Seriki
Press Manager	Martin Shippen
Head of Community	Holly Smith
Technician	Jonathan Strutt
Development Lead	Ines Tercio
Head of Marketing	Ed Theakston
Marketing Officer	Kelly Thurston
Marketing & Development Assistant	Amelia White
General Manager	Camille Wilhelm
Café Bar Manager	Wayne Wilson

DUTY MANAGERS
Sara Dawood, Zak Edwards & Jacob Meier.

VENUE SUPERVISORS
Antony Baker, Adryne Caulder-James, Bo Leandro, Nzuzi Malemba, Chana Nardone & Asa Wooldridge.

VENUE ASSISTANTS
Emma Chatel, Pyerre Clarke, Georgia Fellows, Daniel Fesoom, Matias Hailu, Nzuzi Malemba, Ishani McGuire, Ed Mendoza, Dumo Mkweli, Carys Murray, Louis Nicholson, James Robertson, Manuel Ruis, Ali Shah, Eleanor Stock, Josie Watson, Nefertari Williams, Anna-May Wood & Yemi Yohannes.

BOARD OF TRUSTEES
Uzma Hasan (Chair), Cllr Stala Antionades, Kim Evans, Daisy Heath, Keerthi Kollimada, Taio Lawson, Anthony Marraccino, Jim Marshall, Rajiv Nathwani, Kwame Owusu, Stephen Pidcock, Catherine Score & Angela Wachner.

Bush Theatre, 7 Uxbridge Road, London W12 8LJ
Box Office: 020 8743 5050 | Administration: 020 8743 3584
Email: info@bushtheatre.co.uk | bushtheatre.co.uk

Alternative Theatre Company Ltd
The Bush Theatre is a Registered Charity
and a company limited by guarantee.
Registered in England no. 1221968 Charity no. 270080

THANK YOU

Our supporters make our work possible. Together, we're evolving the canon and creating a bolder, more diverse, and representative future for British theatre. We're so grateful to you all.

MAJOR DONORS
Charles Holloway OBE
Jim & Michelle Gibson
Rajeev Philip
Cathy & Tim Score
Susie Simkins
Jack Thorne
Gianni & Michael Alen-Buckley

SHOOTING STARS
Jim & Michelle Gibson
Anthony Marraccino & Mariela Manso
Cathy & Tim Score
Susie Simkins

LONE STARS
Clyde Cooper
Adam Kenwright
Jim Marshall
Georgia Oetker

HANDFUL OF STARS
Charlie Bigham
Judy Bollinger
Richard & Sarah Clarke
Christopher delaMare
David des Jardins
Sue Fletcher
Thea Guest
Kate Hamer Ltd.
Elizabeth Jack
Simon & Katherine Johnson
Joanna Kennedy
Garry & Lorna Lawrence
Phyllida Lloyd & Kate Pakenham
Vivienne Lukey
Sam & Jim Murgatroyd
Mark & Anne Paterson
Nick & Annie Reid
Bhagat Sharma
Dame Emma Thompson
Joe Tinston & Amelia Knott

RISING STARS
Elizabeth Beebe
Martin Blackburn
David Brooks
Catharine Browne
Anthony Chantry
Lauren Clancy
Caroline Clasen
Susan Cuff
Matthew Cushen
Anne-Hélène and Rafaël Biosse Duplan
Austin Erwin
Kim Evans
Mimi Findlay
Jack Gordon
Hugh & Sarah Grootenhuis
Sarah Harrison
Uzma Hasan
Lesley Hill & Russ Shaw
Davina & Malcolm Judelson
Mike Lewis
Lynette Linton
Tim & Deborah Maunder
Michael McCoy
Judy Mellor
Caro Millington
Rajiv Nathwani
Yoana Nenova
Stephen Pidcock
James St. Ville KC
Jan Topham
Kit & Anthony van Tulleken
Evanna White
Ben Yeoh
Angela Wachner

CORPORATE SPONSORS
Biznography
Casting Pictures Ltd.
Nick Hern Books
S&P Global
The Agency

TRUSTS & FOUNDATIONS
Backstage Trust
Buffini Chao Foundation
Christina Smith Foundation
Daisy Trust
Esmée Fairbairn Foundation
The Foyle Foundation
Garfield Welson Foundation
Garrick Charitable Trust
The Golsoncott Foundation
Hammersmith United Charities
The Harold Hyam Wingate Foundation
Idlewild Trust
Jerwood Foundation
John Lyon's Charity
Martin Bowley Charitable Trust
Noël Coward Foundation
Royal Victorial Hall Foundation
The Thistle Trust

And all the donors who wish to remain anonymous.

If you are interested in finding out how to be involved, please visit **bushtheatre.co.uk/support-us** email **development@bushtheatre.co.uk** or call **020 8743 3584**.

MAGGOTS

Farah Najib

Acknowledgements

Thanks to Soho Theatre for the 2022 residency that gave me the space to begin this story.

Thanks to Chris Thorpe and Jasmine Lee-Jones for their brilliant teaching on a 2023 Arvon retreat, where I explored this idea further – and particularly to Chris for responding to my anxieties about writing a play in prose with, 'well why the fuck not?'

A huge thank you to Fight or Flight Productions for producing an early version of *Maggots* in 2024, and to the Lion & Unicorn Theatre and David Brady for getting it in front of lovely audiences. Thanks too to those who performed so beautifully in that production: Antoinette Harrison, Farah Ashraf and Ross Kernahan.

Thank you to Titilola Dawudu and Lynette Linton for believing in *Maggots* on your way out of the Bush door – it's an honour. And to the current Bush team for continuing to champion the play.

To Jess Barton for your vision, for believing in *Maggots* unwaveringly, and for repeatedly telling me, 'do you know how much I love this script?' at times of doubt.

To Sam Baker Jones, Safiyya Ingar and Marcia Lecky for bringing this story to life with such unwavering warmth, skill and commitment. You three are very talented.

To Jessie Anand for producing with care, rigour and attention to detail.

To my agent Florence Hyde, for helping me get this thing to the stage.

To Annie Chadwick and Yasmine Najib who read very early drafts and encouraged me down the path I was heading.

To my parents and friends for always supporting my journey on this bizarre career path.

And finally to Ross Kernahan, for always being willing to be an unrelenting sounding board when I'm in the weeds with redrafting, helping me untie the knots, and generally being my biggest cheerleader and bringer of cups of tea.

F.N.

'Living well and dying well is a community affair.'

Dr Lydia Dugdale

For anyone who ever wondered: would anyone notice?
Would anyone really notice?

A Note on Inspiration

This play was inspired by true stories of lonely deaths and the systemic failures that allowed them to happen, including those of Sheila Seleoane, Joyce Vincent, Denise Prudhomme, Laura Winham, Robert Alton and Hedviga Golik. There are many, many cases like this. While their stories informed this work, the characters and narrative are wholly fictional. This play is offered in memory of them and the many others who have died alone and gone unnoticed.

A Note on Form

This play uses collaborative storytelling. Three performers share the narrative between them, sometimes stepping into the essence of a character but never fully embodying them. They ghost through these moments rather than perform them. They are storytellers first: warm, present, and engaged with the audience, bringing their own voices, energies, and presence to the work rather than adopting personas. This form allows them to support each other through difficult material and build the world of Laurel House without disappearing into it.

A Note on Language

Lines written in `this font` represent a digital space.

An ellipsis (…) indicates a shift in place, time, and/or story perspective.

Lines with an en dash (–) at the beginning are dialogue and should be treated differently to the third-person storytelling that makes up the main body of the text.

Section titles should be spoken out loud and/or projected (with the exception of Prologue).

A Note on Casting

It's important that the cast features voices representative of the characters in the story.

The names Sam, Safiyya, and Marcia refer to the actors who performed in the January/February 2026 Bush Theatre production. Future productions should substitute the names of their own cast members throughout the text.

This text went to press before the end of rehearsals and so may differ slightly from the play as performed.

Prologue

Three STORYTELLERS *address the audience.*

MARCIA. Hello.

SAM. Hello.

SAFIYYA. Hi.

MARCIA. We're going to tell you a story.

SAFIYYA. We realise that's quite a simplistic way to start our encounter –

SAM. But sometimes, simple is good.

SAFIYYA. This is a story about rot.

SAM. About decay.

MARCIA. About degradation.

They reconsider.

SAFIYYA. It's a story about things falling apart.

They reconsider again.

SAM. It's a story about a life – or lives – crumbling. Disintegrating. Withering away into nothingness.

MARCIA. That sounds quite poetic.

SAM. Thanks.

SAFIYYA. Quite depressing.

SAM. Depends on your sensibilities.

MARCIA. This isn't a story about us.

SAFIYYA. Well – it's not *not* about us.

MARCIA. True. In some ways, it's a story about all of us.

SAM. But this story didn't happen to me.

SAFIYYA. Nor me.

MARCIA. No. Nor me.

SAFIYYA (*to audience*). We've only just met you, we know, but this story, it probably didn't happen to you either.

MARCIA. We hope.

SAM. It could, though. Maybe. With the way things are.

MARCIA. Yes. That's the important part. It could. Depending on who you are, and where you are, and what you are.

SAFIYYA. It's a story with some truth in it.

SAM. But some things –

SAFIYYA. Most things –

SAM. Are completely made up.

SAFIYYA (*by way of explanation*). We're actors.

SAM. If you hadn't guessed.

Maybe they introduce themselves by name.

SAFIYYA. But we're not really going to be playing characters, for the most part.

MARCIA. We're just going to tell you a story.

SAM. Simple as that, really.

A moment. The STORYTELLERS *look to each other, then the audience.*

MARCIA. Ready?

1. A Suspicious Stench

SAM. It is a Thursday morning in July

SAFIYYA. At 4.46 a.m.

SAM. When fifty-eight-year-old Linda Barnes sits on her bed in her flat at number sixty, on the fourth floor of Laurel House –

MARCIA. A small residential block on a quiet street off a busy road in an unremarkable corner of London –

SAM. And types the words into Google:

MARCIA. What does death smell like?

SAFIYYA. Linda *was* getting ready for work –

SAM. And working hard to distract herself with pulling on the scratchy black trousers, shapeless grey T-shirt and blue-and-white striped tunic that make up the uniform for her job as a cleaner of office buildings in the City.

MARCIA. But the smell, which started as a hint two weeks ago but now seems to be seeping from the very walls themselves, has become impossible to ignore.

SAM. Linda finds the scent hard to describe. She's never smelt anything like it before. While video-calling her grown-up and only daughter, Josie –

SAFIYYA. Who lives 10,573 miles away in Sydney, Australia –

SAM. Linda struggles to find the words.

MARCIA. It's kind of… sweet? But not nice sweet. Sweet like fruit that's been left out in the sun for too long. Like an apple that's gone a bit soft on the inside and turned that dark shade of brown that makes you not want to eat the apple.

SAFIYYA. Like sweet, sickly cider.

SAM. But not refreshing. Not like a cold pint of Strongbow on one of these hot summer days. No. It's a sweetness, combined with… something else.

SAFIYYA. Linda doesn't think it smells like death, necessarily. Well. She isn't sure. She's never smelt death before, as far as she's aware.

MARCIA. She's seen dead bodies –

SAM. Her mother.

SAFIYYA. Her father.

MARCIA. More recently, her husband. Clive.

SAM. But that's when they're all… you know. Done up. Smells and unsightliness eradicated.

SAFIYYA. So, she googles it.

MARCIA. What does death smell like? What does a dead body smell like?

SAFIYYA. Linda feels weird, looking that up. What if someone sees her search history?

SAM. What if they're tracking her every move on the internet?

MARCIA. Saying that, she's not really sure who 'they' are, but she still worries that 'they' might know, somehow, what she's been looking up.

SAM. Because they do, don't they? They do look at search histories. And they use them to incriminate people. Linda saw a case like that on Facebook recently, a man who had killed his wife, and they found he'd been looking up all of these awful things online like how to bury a body, how to decompose a body, how long does a body take to start smelling. And he was there in court and they were reading all of that back to him, and he probably thought they couldn't see that, but they could, and the last thing Linda needs right now, the last bloody thing, is for the police to come knocking on her door asking whether she's murdered somebody!

SAFIYYA. Which she hasn't, obviously. When would she have had the time?

MARCIA. So she goes incognito, just to be safe.

We enter a murky online world.

SAM. Linda finds herself in some kind of internet forum.

SAFIYYA. It's called… Reddit?

MARCIA. Someone compares the smell to rotten eggs or sewage.

SAFIYYA. Someone else describes it as having fruity undertones. As if it's wine. Or perfume.

MARCIA. Another person writes that the bacteria produced by death is known to cling to your nostril hairs and multiply later. Meaning you'll carry on smelling it, even when you're not around the smell any more.

SAM. Someone else says it's like a butcher's shop on a hot day. Like meat that's just…

SAFIYYA. Rotting

And rotting

And rotting away.

MARCIA. Someone else says they *like* the smell. That's when Linda decides to get off the internet because she feels sick to the pit of her stomach, and she's going to be late for work.

We leave the online world.

…

Every day for the next week, Linda rides the Tube in silent solidarity with the other baggy-eyed, early-morning workers – all of them sweating like pigs.

SAM. This is one of the hottest Julys in London memory.

SAFIYYA. At work, she goes through the usual routine of hoovering corporate carpet tiles

Wiping splatters of spag-bol from communal microwaves

Dusting desks adorned with framed family photos

And bleaching bog bowls smeared with City of London shit.

MARCIA. But all she can think about is –

SAM. That smell. The one that's still there every time she gets home. Her daughter, Josie, suggests the communal rubbish area could be to blame, made worse by the heatwave.

MARCIA. But it isn't like any bins Linda's smelt –

SAM. And Linda's smelt a lot of bins.

…

SAFIYYA. The Laurel House tenants' group chat is, generally speaking, used less for socialising or idle chit-chat, and more for practical matters, like –

SAM. Hi everyone, just a heads-up that the lock on the bin shed is broken again. Have reported it. [Thumbs-up emoji]

SAFIYYA. Hi folks, does anyone know if there are normal bin collections happening during the Christmas week? [Thinking-face emoji]

MARCIA. Please if it isn't any trouble could someone move their bike from the third-floor corridor, have tripped over it three times now. Thanks appreciate it. [Winking-face emoji, hands-raised-in-celebration emoji]

SAFIYYA. You get the idea. Messages of dry necessity. Uninspiring practicality. British politeness or passive aggression. But not so much on the Thursday evening –

MARCIA. 8.17 p.m. –

SAFIYYA. That Linda decides to reach out.

SAM (*as* LINDA). Hi everyone. Sorry for the weird message but has anyone noticed a dodgy smell lately?

MARCIA. Carly Lewis –

SAM. Who lives two doors down from Linda at number sixty-two –

MARCIA. Had, in fact, noticed a dodgy smell lately.

SAM. Carly lives with her six-month-old. Noah.

SAFIYYA. Noah means 'rest'. Ironically, he doesn't rest at all. So, neither can Carly.

MARCIA. At just twenty-three, some would call Carly a baby herself. She's a single mum, or as she prefers to call it, a double-mum. Her mum-ness isn't defined by her relationship status, it's defined by how much work she does as a mum, and being a single mum, she does double the fucking work.

SAFIYYA. Carly has to be a double-mum, because Noah's daddy is a completely useless, jobless man-child with a commitment problem and a dick the size of her little finger.

SAM. He went running for the hills the very day he saw those little blue lines.

MARCIA. Her parents said, we told you so. You'll ruin your life. We're not going to bail you out this time.

But she went ahead with it anyway. And they haven't really spoken since.

SAM. Carly is into the spiritual stuff. Her small flat is filled with brightly coloured pillows, patterned throws, fairy lights, elephant ornaments, tasselled rugs.

SAFIYYA. It's giving 'gap year in Bali', except Carly never got to go on a gap year, and hasn't left the UK since a family holiday to Mallorca when she was thirteen.

MARCIA. To relax, Carly likes to burn shit. Sage sticks, incense, scented candles.

SAM. And yeah, alright, sometimes when she *really* needs to relax, she *might* light up something stronger, out on the balcony, when she's finally managed to get Noah to sleep.

SAFIYYA. *If* she's managed to get Noah to sleep.

SAM. Just to take the edge off, you know? It's basically aromatherapy, anyway.

MARCIA. Carly has just taken the first delicious drag of one such balcony relaxation session when her phone pings with Linda's message. *Has anyone noticed a dodgy smell lately?*

SAFIYYA (*as* CARLY). Actually I have yeah. What is that? Smells gross.

SAM. Something that not even the thick, heady scents of nag champa or lavender or sandalwood or Super Lemon Haze could completely disguise.

SAFIYYA (*as* CARLY). The binmen aren't on strike again are they? I didn't get a leaflet through.

MARCIA. Linda –

SAM. Sprawled on the sofa with a decrepit old fan blowing a pathetic breeze at her ankles –

MARCIA. Blinks down at her phone.

SAM (*as* LINDA). I don't think they are on strike, no.

MARCIA. And, finally, the thing she hasn't wanted to ask.

SAM (*as* LINDA). Have you seen number sixty-one lately?

Beat.

MARCIA. Linda and Carly know next-to-nothing about each other, but even less about number sixty-one, the woman they share a wall with. They exchange pleasantries and half-smiles and half-nods and you-alrights and not much more than that.

SAM. Carly's head swims.

SAFIYYA (*as* CARLY). I haven't in a bit you know. I can normally hear her through the wall.

MARCIA. Nobody else replies.

2. A Frustrating Interaction

SAM. The next morning –

MARCIA. Hiding in a shiny bathroom cubicle of a Broadgate Circle office building –

SAM. Linda phones the housing.

We enter an absurd, bureaucratic world.

MARCIA. – It's a funny smell. In the corridors. And in my flat.

SAFIYYA. – What kind of a funny smell

MARCIA. – I'm not sure, it's hard to describe. It just smells… off.

SAFIYYA. – Off

MARCIA. – Yes. Off. Weird.

SAFIYYA. – Riiiight have the binmen gone on strike again

MARCIA. – You're asking me? Shouldn't you know that?

SAFIYYA. – I dunno

MARCIA. – You dunno?

SAFIYYA. – No sorryyy

MARCIA. – Erm, okay, well – I don't think it's the bins.

SAFIYYA. – Okaaay ermmm have you tried opening a window

MARCIA. – Opening a window?

SAFIYYA. – Yesss opening a window in your flat

MARCIA. – Yes, of course, but I don't think that's… the smell isn't coming from outside.

SAFIYYA. – Riiiight where do you think it's coming from then

A pause.

MARCIA. – We haven't seen our neighbour at number sixty-one in a while.

SAFIYYA. – Okaaay and what's that got to do with the smell

MARCIA. – Do I really have to spell it out for you?

SAFIYYA. – Weeeeell if you wouldn't mind, I'm not a mind-reader Mrs Barnes

MARCIA. – I – I'm just wondering. What if she's, you know?

SAFIYYA. – What if she's whaaaat

MARCIA. – Dead. What if she's dead?

Beat. Laughter.

SAFIYYA. She won't be deeeead will she

MARCIA. – Sorry, but how do you know?

SAFIYYA. – It's a bit over-the-top isn't it

Have you tried knocking on her door

MARCIA. – Er – no.

SAFIYYA. – Weeeell maybe give that a go first then, ay

Call disconnects.

SAM. The next morning. Linda's first Saturday off in bloody weeks! But instead of what she had planned –

SAFIYYA. Reclining on the sofa in her dressing gown watching *Saturday Kitchen* and perving on that Matt Tebbutt –

MARCIA. Cor, he's a dish –

SAM. She's standing in front of number sixty-one's door, heart near hammering out of her chest, and wondering when she became so…

SAFIYYA. So…

SAM. *Not* Clive.

MARCIA. Linda's late husband was a people-person. The force of exuberant friendliness and total lack of social boundaries he brought to a room was ridiculous –

SAFIYYA. And incredible.

SAM. He wasn't perfect. At times, Clive liked people –

MARCIA. Liked *women* –

SAM. A bit too much. Never a full-blown affair –

MARCIA. At least, not that Linda knew of –

SAM. But there was a wandering eye, a drunken snog down the pub, a naughty text sent at 2 a.m.

MARCIA. It was the way he looked at her the morning after, though. Like Linda was the only person in the world who mattered. Like he was genuinely sorry. Like he'd never do it again.

SAFIYYA. So, she forgave him. Once, twice, three times. It was that bloody relentless charm of his. It's not like he set out to hurt her. He simply couldn't help himself. And what was the alternative? Being alone?

MARCIA. Ironic, then, that she ended up alone nonetheless. Selfish of him, really, after all her tolerance, for him to drop dead of a heart attack on the eve of their thirtieth wedding anniversary.

Beat.

SAM. Despite his misdemeanours, Clive made Linda brave. More willing to step outside her comfort zone. But nowadays, she only felt…

MARCIA. Frightened. Frightened of everything.

SAFIYYA. Frightened of life.

SAM. So when she does eventually force herself to knock on the cold, plain, white wood of number sixty-one's door, it is the lightest *rap-rap-rap* she can muster.

The STORYTELLERS *wait. Nothing.*

MARCIA. Linda knocks again, more confidently this time.

They wait. Still nothing.

SAFIYYA. Once more. Three hard, loud knocks. Couldn't miss 'em.

They wait again.

MARCIA. Nothing. Nobody.

Beat.

As Linda stands there, her nose is greeted by two smells. The first being the unmistakeably pungent herbal scent floating from beneath number sixty-two's door.

SAFIYYA. She checks her watch. Christ – it's only 10 a.m. And she can hear a baby crying.

MARCIA. And the other is that sweet meat stench, now undeniably from number sixty-one, seeping insidiously into her nostrils –

SAM. No doubt doing exactly what the internet said it would and clinging to the little hairs inside –

SAFIYYA. Which, Linda has noticed, seemed to be growing thicker and darker with each passing year.

…

MARCIA. Another week passes.

SAM. Linda phones the housing again

And again

And again.

MARCIA. Eventually, a weaselly young man named Darren –

SAM (*cocky*). Job title: Neighbourhood Manager –

MARCIA. Makes an appearance at Laurel House.

SAFIYYA. Darren. Fresh off the back of a business studies degree –

SAM. 2:2 –

SAFIYYA. ID badge shiny and new. Gormless, smiling mugshot stamped on the front.

MARCIA. Cheap suit hanging off him like a little boy in his daddy's clothes.

SAFIYYA. Darren stands in the corridor with his hands on his skinny hips, looking back at the concerned faces of Linda and Carly, who has Noah asleep in her arms.

MARCIA. The sight of his cherub-like face produces a strange feeling in Linda's chest. She thinks of when Josie was small. Wonders if Josie will ever have a baby of her own. Finds herself gripped by the overwhelming need to hold Noah.

SAFIYYA. Her reverie is shattered by Darren saying things like –

SAM. – You lot aren't doing the bins properly again, are you? We've told you about this.

SAFIYYA. And –

SAM. – Maybe it's the damp. It's the damp again, no doubt.

MARCIA. And –

SAM. – It's probably the drains, isn't it? Drains smell horrible. They do smell like death. It's just London, isn't it! Dirty and disgusting – especially in this heat. Not much we can do about it, unfortunately! It's just the city.

MARCIA. Linda, not wanting to wake Noah, whispers angrily back that she doesn't think it is the bins, or the damp, or the drains, actually.

SAFIYYA. Undeterred, Darren strides confidently over to the one and only corridor window, which is already open to its maximum two inches –

MARCIA. It's one of those safety windows.

SAFIYYA. He tugs at it pointlessly.

SAM. – See that? Fresh air! Lovely.

MARCIA. The air is hot, stagnant, and anything but lovely.

SAM. – Keep this place aired. We'll take a look into it.

SAFIYYA. Darren goes to leave. Carly steps in his path.

MARCIA. Linda likes that. Brave.

SAFIYYA. Carly's gaze locks onto Darren. They are nose to nose.

SAM. Her eyes are like, so blue... and bloodshot. Is she stoned or just knackered? She's pretty, though... really pretty. Oh great, now he's blushing. For fuck's sake, Darren, you're such a fucking loser.

SAFIYYA. – What about number sixty-one, Darren?

She doesn't like being so close to this pathetic excuse for a man. Sour breath. Bad skin. Too much Lynx Africa.

MARCIA. Darren's mole-like pupils flit to that cold, plain, white wood door, only for a second, but Carly doesn't miss the flash of fear in his eyes.

SAM. – She's still paying her rent, so she must be alright.

SAFIYYA. And with that, he leaves.

3. Overbrimming Post and Unwelcome Pests

MARCIA. Another week passes –

SAFIYYA. Just about long enough for the stench of Lynx Africa to fade from the corridors.

MARCIA. It's Friday morning, 8.02 a.m., when fifteen-year-old Jaydn Abiola is hanging around in the foyer of Laurel House –

SAM. Where he lives with his mum Rebecca at flat fifty, on the third floor. The one *below* Linda, Carly, and number sixty-one.

SAFIYYA. His mum will kill him if she finds out he isn't already halfway to school, but who cares, man, it's last week of term anyway.

SAM. And his next-door neighbour Aleena usually leaves for college around now, and yeah, she has already told Jaydn that she is not going to go on a date with him, because he is fifteen years old and she is eighteen years old –

SAFIYYA. And where the fuck would he take her anyway, he doesn't have a job or any money –

SAM. But he can't help but try.

SAFIYYA. It's while he's in the foyer trying to get eyes on Aleena that his eye is caught by the letterbox for number sixty-one, which has bare letters in it. There are some white envelopes, and a few brown ones too.

MARCIA. Jaydn knows that brown envelopes are the bad ones. His mum is never happy when she has a brown envelope to open.

SAM. He wonders for a moment why the woman at number sixty-one isn't collecting her post. That lady he sees at the bus stop sometimes. But the thought is interrupted by the sound of the lift coming down, and his heart lurches into his stomach.

MARCIA. He quickly wets two fingers to smooth down his eyebrows, which his mum says are unusually unruly for a boy of his age.

SAFIYYA. He positions himself in front of the lift doors, trying and failing to strike the kind of pose that looks natural –

MARCIA. Nonchalant –

SAM. Completely unbothered.

MARCIA. But when the doors slide open, he's greeted not by the fine form of Aleena, but by Rebecca instead, in her work uniform, and she has a face like thunder when she sees him standing there.

SAFIYYA. Allow it, man.

MARCIA. She steps out angrily, asking him what the bloody hell is he still doing here, he left for school fifteen minutes ago, and so why is she seeing him lingering about in this here corridor? He better not be trying to chat up that Aleena girl again, she's already told him, she isn't interested, and he needs to accept that!

SAM. Jaydn's face flushes. His mum always knows how to shame him.

SAFIYYA. But it's last week of term!

MARCIA. Rebecca does not care about last week of term. Every minute counts if he wants to pass his GCSEs next year. He isn't going to become 'black Brian Cox' –

SAFIYYA. Jaydn's words –

MARCIA. Without knuckling down.

SAFIYYA. Jaydn loves science. Physics, specifically. Obsessed with getting lost thinking about galaxies and stars and all that massive unknown space.

MARCIA. Rebecca marches him out of the foyer and onto the pavement, eyeballing the back of his head to ensure he is going in the direction of school –

SAM. And wishing she had given him a kiss goodbye despite her irritation.

MARCIA. What a horror it is, as a parent, to have your heart go walking around outside your body.

And why can't the lazy good-for-nothings in this building collect their post?

...

SAM. Forty-one-year-old Rebecca Abiola is a care home nurse. With all the time she spends wiping old people's arses, she barely has time to wipe her own –

MARCIA. Let alone pay attention to a silly group chat that she didn't want to be in, anyway.

SAM. Doing what she does, Rebecca is used to bad smells.

SAFIYYA. Medicine and bleach and shit and piss and illness and ageing and sometimes –

SAM. Often –

SAFIYYA. Death.

SAM. But fresh death. Not... rot.

SAFIYYA. So she hasn't spent much time thinking about the funny smell in the corridors.

MARCIA. But that evening, as Rebecca prepares to leave for her night shift, Jaydn sits at the kitchen table flicking through his chemistry revision pack and recounting an experiment he did at school that day.

SAFIYYA. Sulphur dioxide, Mum. You should've *smelt* that. It's like rotten eggs and farts, you know. Or, I dunno, like... something dead. I swear I can still smell it.

SAM. Rebecca watches her son wrinkle his nose in confusion and realises that the reason he thinks he can still smell it –

MARCIA. Is because he can.

Beat.

SAFIYYA. With a sinking feeling, she remembers that woman from upstairs –

MARCIA. Linda, is it?

SAFIYYA. Sent a message nearly three weeks ago now. *Has anyone seen number sixty-one lately?*

MARCIA (*as* REBECCA). I can smell something nasty down here too. And sixty-one's letterbox is full.

...

SAFIYYA. It is the following Monday at 8.04 p.m. when forty-nine-year-old Adeel Bakash –

SAM. Flat fifty-one, next door to Rebecca and Jaydn –

SAFIYYA. Stands on a chair to change his living-room lightbulb, which has been flickering for a week. 8.04 p.m. Four minutes after the end of *EastEnders* and those satisfying doof-doof-doofs that never fail to fill Adeel's heart with excitement, even after thirty years in the UK.

SAM. If you ask Adeel, first best thing about the UK: the NHS. Second best thing: *EastEnders*.

SAFIYYA. His teenage daughter Aleena –

SAM. Object of Jaydn's affections –

SAFIYYA. Always jokes that *EastEnders* is, like, mega-haraam, and if Adeel died right there on the sofa watching it, he'd be going straight to the bad place for a very tough punishment.

MARCIA. But – the lightbulb.

SAFIYYA. Yes – the lightbulb. Adeel hadn't gotten around to changing it, because every day for the past week as he walked home from his job as a pharmacy assistant, he forgot to pop into the hardware shop to buy the bulb.

MARCIA. That Monday, he remembered, but only because he'd passed underneath a flickering streetlight.

SAM. As Adeel drags the rickety kitchen chair into the living room, Aleena says to him –

SAFIYYA. Be careful, Dad, the legs on these chairs are shit.

MARCIA. Adeel knows! It's alright!

SAM. But Aleena stands behind him with her arms outstretched anyway, in a way that suggests she'll catch him if he falls –

SAFIYYA. Even though she probably won't, because although her father is small in height, in the last year he has discovered those Cadbury's chocolate digestives with that sticky caramel layer in the middle. And that discovery, joyous as it has been, has now shown itself in the tightness of his trousers and the number on the scales.

MARCIA. Adeel jokes that there's more of him to love –

SAFIYYA. Which Aleena doesn't really get, considering her mother –

MARCIA. Layla –

SAFIYYA. Died two years prior. And he hasn't looked at another woman since.

Beat.

SAM. But still, Aleena stands.

MARCIA. Adeel, atop wobbly wooden legs and his own creaky but still functioning legs, unscrews the finished-with lightbulb and hands it to his daughter, who hands him the new one, freshly unboxed.

SAM. Adeel turns back to the light fitting, now bereft of its bulb, open and waiting, and out of it crawls –

SAFIYYA. A maggot.

A single maggot.

The STORYTELLERS *pause. They themselves are horrified.*

MARCIA. Adeel yelps.

SAM. The shit wooden chair legs wobble.

MARCIA. He falls backwards, and instead of catching her father, instead of softening his fall –

SAM. Aleena unconsciously leaps to the side to avoid him altogether –

SAFIYYA. And Adeel comes crashing to the floor.

MARCIA. Presumably startled too, the single maggot falls from the light fitting, landing silently atop Adeel's curving belly. Father and daughter stare at it in horror. Aleena says –

SAFIYYA. Eww, Dad, what the actual fuck?

…

SAM. It is this moment –

MARCIA. Obviously –

SAM. That prompts Adeel to finally reply to the messages on the Laurel House tenants' group chat.

SAFIYYA (*as* ADEEL). `I haven't seen her in ages either`

`A maggot just came through my ceiling`

`Is she dead`

`LOL`

A moment.

SAM. Adeel's heart sinks. What was he thinking?

He stares at the group chat for the rest of the evening, anxiously shovelling McVitie's into his mouth.

Nobody replies.

...

SAFIYYA. It spreads.

Beat.

SAM. Linda is brewing a cup of builder's and blasting Magic FM when a cluster of them is suddenly there, without warning, on the kitchen windowsill. Mere inches from the pink, porcelain, pig-shaped biscuit jar gifted to her by Clive on her fiftieth birthday.

SAFIYYA. Carly is taking advantage of Noah's naptime to flow through some rushed living room sun salutations when a trio appears at the end of her yoga mat. Just sitting. Gently wriggling.

MARCIA. Jaydn turns a page in Stephen Hawking's *A Brief History of Time,* which he is attempting to read for the third time –

SAFIYYA. Man he loves physics, but *man* this book is confusing –

MARCIA. To find a pair, just there, hanging out on the page, partially concealing a passage about black holes and the event horizon.

SAFIYYA. Aleena is getting ready for a house party when she spots one lingering, completely nonchalant, by her make-up bag.

SAM. As if waiting to doll itself up.

MARCIA. And Rebecca is dancing in her living room, as she likes to do once a fortnight when Jaydn is visiting his father –

SAM. From whom Rebecca has been *amicably separated* for six years now. He does his bit for Jaydn, she'll give him that. But she's the one doing the actual raising.

SAFIYYA. These visits offer rare slices of freedom.

MARCIA. She moves to the sweet sounds of Miss Susan Cadogan and sips her weekly measure of dark rum.

'Hurt so Good' by Susan Cadogan plays.

She is feeling good, good for the first time in a while –

SAFIYYA. When a cluster appears in the corner of her ceiling.

MARCIA. She screams blue murder. The glass drops. The precious rum is wasted.

Beat.

SAM. Maggots appear in corridors

SAFIYYA. Maggots appear on balconies

MARCIA. Maggots appear on windowsills

SAM. In showers

SAFIYYA. On sofas

MARCIA. On bookshelves

SAM. In cupboards

SAFIYYA. And carpets

SAM. In the parts of these places that these people call home

And from underneath the door of number sixty-one.

SAFIYYA. Squirming writhing wriggling jiggling

SAM. Twitching turning snaking worming

MARCIA. Slinking slithering crawling creeping feeding festering

Maggots.

SAM (*as* LINDA). There are maggots in my home

MARCIA (*as* REBECCA). Mine too

SAFIYYA (*as* CARLY). Mine too

What the fuck is going on?

4. Another Frustrating Interaction Not With Darren But One of the Others from the Housing Who Behaves Very Fucking Similarly to Darren

Another phone call. The absurd, bureaucratic world.

MARCIA. – What do you mean, they don't do maggots?

SAM. – Pest control they don't do maggots

MARCIA. – Why not?

SAM. – Not sure… too wriggly?

MARCIA. – Sorry – what are we supposed to do then?

SAM. – You'll have to deal with them yourself I suppose

MARCIA. – How?

Typing.

SAM. – Says online you can pour boiling water on them… or a fifty-fifty bleach and water mix… or squeeze lemon juice on them… or sprinkle salt over them

MARCIA. – Salt?

SAM. – Yes salt table salt not rock salt

MARCIA. – What does salt do?

SAM. – Dehydrates them to death apparently

MARCIA (*horrified*). – Oh.

SAM. – Careful though… says here the tiny maggots die quickly but the big ones can take up to eight hours

MARCIA (*more horrified*). – Eight hours?

SAM. – That's right yeah how big are they your maggots

MARCIA. – They're not *my* maggots. But they're… a variety of sizes. And it's not just me. It's other tenants, too.

SAM. – Right okay well I suppose you best sprinkle liberally then

A chuckle.

– Says here a group of maggots is called a grumble… how funny

MARCIA. – They're coming through the ceiling. And there are flies, too. Do they do flies, pest control?

Flicking through paper.

SAM. – No they don't do flies either I'm afraid

MARCIA. – Why not?

SAM. – I'm not sure… I suppose they'd be hard to catch wouldn't they, being flies

MARCIA. – Well what do pest control do then?

More flicking.

SAM. – Mice rats cockroaches bedbugs termites mosquitoes wasps spiders pigeons foxes ants flying ants

MARCIA. – Hang on – they don't do flies, but they *do* do flying ants?

SAM. – That's what it says

Silence.

MARCIA. – Look, can you just send Darren over again? We need to speak to him.

Beat.

SAM. – …who?

MARCIA. – …Darren? Our neighbourhood manager? I thought he was on this case.

Typing.

SAM. – Oh right yeah Darren he's off on holiday I'm afraid. Cyprus. Alright for some ain't it

MARCIA. – Right. What am I supposed to do then? What are *we* supposed to do? And what about our neighbour? What about number sixty-one?

Call disconnects.

…

(*As* LINDA.) I think we need to meet.

SAM. The following evening, the grown-ups gather in Linda's cramped living room. The whole thing feels…

SAFIYYA. Uncomfortable. Awkward, even. They haven't done this before.

SAM. And yet, it's remarkable how easy it was to get people together. Just one text.

SAFIYYA. Adeel, Carly and baby Noah squeeze onto Linda's beige two-seater, which has seen better days.

MARCIA. Rebecca stays standing, rubbing her lower back impatiently. She's sore and she's tired and she doesn't want to be here. Her one night off all week!

That little bubba is very cute, though. But my god, how young is his mother?

SAM. Linda makes tea, and offers biscuits from the pink, porcelain, pig-shaped biscuit jar.

SAFIYYA. Rich teas, ugh! Not up to Adeel's standards –

SAM. But he still eats four.

MARCIA. Rebecca declines the tea –

SAFIYYA. Thinking desperately of her rum –

MARCIA. And surveys Linda's flat with thinly-veiled judgement. She seems to be a collector of… knick-knacks. The pig biscuit jar, the cat-shaped teapot –

And an entire glass cabinet dedicated to displaying a collection of bizarre novelty items.

Decorative thimbles. Brightly coloured egg cups. Commemorative coronation plates. A ceramic duck.

SAFIYYA. Each trinket and ornament is perfectly polished and placed with so much care. With so much love.

MARCIA. But they are… ugly. Extremely ugly.

Beat.

SAM. The group exchanges the smallest of talk.

SAFIYYA. Gosh, it was a hot July, wasn't it.

MARCIA. Too hot, if you ask me.

SAM. We'll miss it when it's gone, won't we. When those dark nights come back in.

SAFIYYA. No, you're right. You're right.

MARCIA. This is Noah, is it? Oh, hello, Noah.

SAM. How's work?

SAFIYYA. How's the flat?

MARCIA. How's… things?

> They want to talk about what to do. What action to take. How angry they are. And scared.

SAM. But they're not sure how.

SAFIYYA. Eventually, Linda bursts out with –

SAM. What if we break down her door?

> What? If they won't do it, why shouldn't we?

MARCIA. As Linda says this, she's not even sure if she means it.

SAFIYYA. A heavy silence fills the room.

SAM. Adeel considers this possibility, and then thinks quite suddenly of his dead wife. Layla. And the light behind her eyes. That luminous light he fell deliriously in love with at age twenty. Then, he thinks of how it felt to watch that light slip slowly away. To look into her eyes as she lay in the hospice bed and see nothing but grey.

> He mumbles, I'm not so sure.

SAFIYYA. Rebecca is picturing the elderly man she was dealing with just today, and how, although he wasn't dead yet, he looked it.

MARCIA. Nah. I'm not doing that. That's not my job. And I am not getting done for breaking and entering.

SAM. In her mind all she can think is: this isn't work. These aren't my residents.

MARCIA. Linda looks to Carly, who flounders.

SAFIYYA. But what if she's fine?

> Yeah! What if she's fine? Imagine! Imagine if we do that – we break down her door, and everything's fine and she's just sat there chilling on the sofa watching TV. What then? That would be so awkward.

MARCIA. Noah giggles. Even he knows what Carly is saying is nonsense.

SAM. Linda asks herself –

What would a braver person do? What would Clive do?

SAFIYYA. She knows full well what he would do.

SAM. But she is not a braver person. And she cannot do it alone.

A moment.

MARCIA. So that's that.

SAM. They agree on nothing.

SAFIYYA. They decide to do… nothing.

5. The Bit Inbetween

SAM. Here are some things that happen during this time.

SAFIYYA. A man visits Laurel House to check everyone's gas, and when number sixty-one doesn't answer, he sticks a notice to the door and leaves.

MARCIA. The oppressive heatwave gradually relents. The summer holidays come to an end. September. Jaydn starts Year 11 – GCSEs.

SAFIYYA. Big man.

SAM. He reckons.

MARCIA. Aleena, having received her A-level results and passing with flying colours –

SAFIYYA. Obviously –

MARCIA. Secures her place at Cambridge to study NatSci.

SAFIYYA. Natural Sciences. Specialise in Chemistry, then a PhD, then become a research scientist. Aleena *is* going to cure cancer.

SAM. But she decides to defer –

SAFIYYA. The dead mum card will get you everywhere –

MARCIA. And embark on a gap year, of sorts.

SAFIYYA. Adeel does not understand this phrase, 'gap year'. What gap? Why gap? This was never the plan. A girl as clever as Aleena! Why waste time?

SAM. She keeps saying she wants to find herself, but she isn't going travelling, so where exactly is she hoping to find herself between the high street, the Tube, and TikTok?

MARCIA. Really, Aleena just wants to stay home a little bit longer.

SAM. The sweet meat stench intensifies, changes, warps. Towels are wedged under doors. Glade air fresheners are purchased. Carly invests in increasingly obscure incense sticks that don't even denote any particular kind of smell –

SAFIYYA. 'Dragon's Blood.'

MARCIA. 'Sunrise.'

SAFIYYA. 'Positive Vibes.'

MARCIA. Linda makes twelve phone calls to the housing.

SAFIYYA. October. The welcome chill and warm orange hues of autumn.

SAM (*spooky*). Halloweeeeeen. Jaydn goes trick or treating with his mates, dressed up as a skeleton.

MARCIA. Which Rebecca finds to be in poor taste.

SAM. The housing puts up an Instagram story wishing their tenants a Happy Halloween, accompanied by a gif of some zombies.

MARCIA. Which Rebecca finds to be in even poorer taste.

SAFIYYA. Aleena posts a TikTok of herself doing a viral dance in a sexy cat costume. Classic Halloween look.

SAM. She only uploads it in the hope that *she* will see it...

ALL (*dreamy*). Maya.

SAFIYYA. But somehow, it blows up. 785,000 views.

MARCIA. Twenty-eight phone calls to the housing.

SAM. Christmas.

   Linda's favourite holiday – or, used to be. She and Clive were unstoppable. Linda on turkey –

MARCIA. Never dry –

SAM. Clive on veg. Honey-roasted parsnips, cauliflower cheese, Buttery, bacon-y brussels that probably took years off his life. Now, Linda sits alone and Facetimes Australia. It's sunny and hot there. All wrong, on Christmas! Josie asks whether they're dealing with it.

MARCIA. No, love. They're not.

   Jaydn has Christmas at his dad's. Rebecca is working – time and a half. Needs the money.

SAM. Carly receives a two-word text from her dad: Happy Christmas. She doesn't reply.

SAFIYYA. For Adeel and Aleena, it's just another day.

MARCIA. New Year's Eve! Fireworks. What feels like the whole city celebrating, except at Laurel House.

SAM. Forty-five phone calls.

SAFIYYA. January. Drudgery. Grey.

MARCIA. Darren resurfaces. Gets in touch with Linda, who has become the unofficial –

SAFIYYA. And involuntary –

MARCIA. Residents' spokesperson.

SAM. He's back from Cyprus. Lovely weather.

MARCIA. Must've been a very long holiday.

SAM. We're looking into it, he says. Still looking into it.

SAFIYYA. Linda shares this update in the Laurel House tenants' group chat, used less for socialising or idle chit-chat, and more for practical matters –

SAM. Like whether your neighbour is dead.

MARCIA (*as* LINDA). Darren phoned. Still looking into it, apparently.

SAM. Days pass, no replies. And then, Adeel.

SAFIYYA (*as* ADEEL). Maybe she just likes to keep herself to herself.

Beat.

MARCIA. February. Valentine's. Adeel looks through photos of his Layla. His light.

SAFIYYA. And he cooks, furiously, trying to fill his flat with the aromas that remind him of back home. Anywhere but here. But it's pointless. Everything tastes like ash – even his famous biryani.

SAM. Sixty-eight calls.

MARCIA. Carly, instead of being loved, slumps on the sofa, half-baked and half-watching *Gogglebox* whilst mindlessly swiping through her friends' Instagram stories, where they show off what they're doing with *their* Valentine's nights. Cocktail glasses clinking together –

SAFIYYA. 'Galentine's forever!'

MARCIA. Or a hand being held across a candlelit table –

SAFIYYA. 'Valentine's with this one, couldn't hope for anything more.'

MARCIA. But it's also Noah's first birthday. He's not so much a baby any more but a small, wobbly person. They share a tiny cake. Carly helps him to blow out the candle and makes a wish for none of this to be real.

SAM. Jaydn stalks Aleena's Insta feed.

SAFIYYA. Aleena stalks Maya's Insta feed.

MARCIA. Rebecca –

SAM. In an act entirely out of character –

MARCIA. Downloads a dating app and begins exchanging messages with a very, very sexy man named Darnell.

SAM. March. Linda relentlessly looks up prices of flights to Sydney, Australia.

SAFIYYA. April. Ramadan rolls around. The fast. Adeel is barely eating, anyway. How can he? His biscuit belly is as good as gone.

SAM. His cousins in Birmingham phone non-stop. Come for Eid, bring Aleena. But Adeel makes his excuses. Next year, maybe.

SAFIYYA. Eighty-nine calls.

MARCIA. May. A dark wave of guilt and unease begins to flood Rebecca's psyche. She takes on extra shifts. Double shifts, triple shifts. Anything to distract. Her once-a-week rum treat bleeds out to other days. She tries to help Jaydn revise for his GCSEs.

SAFIYYA. But she cannot focus. The words swim and squirm on the page, like –

SAM. Like maggots.

MARCIA. One night, she skives off work to meet up with Darnell. They have quick, feverish sex in the back of his car. She needs to feel alive. It's the first time she's been touched in seven years.

SAFIYYA. At the end of another sleep-deprived, zombie-like day, Adeel quietly slips a packet of sleeping tablets into his pocket at work. That night, he takes one, then – frightened by his own thoughts – flushes the rest down the toilet.

SAM. Carly smokes more and begins to feel paranoid that a strange woman is going to steal Noah from his cot in the middle of the night.

MARCIA. One hundred and two.

SAM. June. Jaydn's exams roll around and they are really, really hard. The image of his future disintegrates in front of his eyes. He is too scared to even tell his mum –

MARCIA. Who'll be damned if she sees her son get caught up in nonsense like the other boys.

SAFIYYA. One hundred and twenty-three.

MARCIA. Nobody really speaks to one another. The group chat goes even quieter than it was before. No mundane messages about bins or bikes.

SAFIYYA. The police do come. Welfare check. But even they won't break down her door. No just cause, they say.

SAM. Darren doesn't come round again. Nobody comes round again.

SAFIYYA. Linda tots up one hundred and fifty-seven phone calls to the housing.

SAM. Linda also falls into something like a depression, although she doesn't like that word.

MARCIA. People can barely make eye contact in the corridors. They look down at their phones, the floor, anywhere but each other's faces.

SAM. If they look, they might see the same guilt reflected back at them. The same fear. The same terrible complicity.

Beat.

SAFIYYA. During this time, everyone dreams.

SAM. Of maggots

MARCIA. And of dirt

SAFIYYA. And of bodies being left to rot.

MARCIA. During this time, number sixty-one's gas is cut off, but nobody enters her flat

SAM. Number sixty-one stops paying rent, but nobody enters her flat

SAFIYYA. Number sixty-one doesn't respond to notices, but nobody enters her flat

SAM. Number sixty-one doesn't respond to knocks

To phone calls

To emails

But nobody enters her flat. The door remains firmly closed.

SAFIYYA. Something that Linda thinks a lot during this time is –

Why isn't anyone looking for her?

MARCIA. And –

It could be me.

ALL. It could be me.

SAM. There is nobody to check on me any more.

Husband gone. Daughter miles away.

MARCIA. Would anyone notice?

Would anyone really notice?

6. The Finding

A thunderstorm.

SAFIYYA. It is a Tuesday morning in July –

SAM. One year on –

SAFIYYA. When a loud sound pulls Carly Lewis violently out of sleep at 2.17 a.m. The sound is not the usual sound that wakes Carly in the night – Noah stirring. No, tonight that isn't it.

MARCIA. The awakening feels awful. Carly doesn't understand how you don't get used to it after having a baby. Every single time feels like a large, unfriendly hand grasping you by the neck, yanking you from the dark trenches of dreamless sleep, and slinging you, crashing you, down into wakefulness.

SAFIYYA. It feels like shit.

SAM. And it feels even worse tonight, because it could be said that Carly had had a few white wines that evening. It's not like she'd been out or anything, but she was trying to kick the weed, due to the crippling paranoia that had taken hold. But she still needed something to take the edge off –

SAFIYYA. Obviously –

SAM. So, wine. The cheapest she can get.

SAFIYYA. I mean, how different can it be? It's just grapes.

MARCIA. That night she sits, and drinks, and plans fake adventures for herself on Google Maps –

SAM. Cambodia. Vietnam. Thailand. The Phillipines.

MARCIA. And she thinks about how, in a way, her life has been stolen from her, and maybe her parents were right when they said she wasn't ready for this, maybe it's true, maybe she should've –

Beat.

SAFIYYA. And then she feels terrible for thinking that. Just awful. Like the worst person in the world. But there's nothing to do and nobody to speak to except a toddler, who she loves very much but *fucking hell*.

SAM. So why not have another glass?

MARCIA. In the couple of hours Carly had been asleep, a hangover had started to creep in, characterised by a dry, cottony tongue and a deep throbbing in her skull. Her body is clammy. Her pyjamas stick to her like glue.

SAFIYYA. It takes her a moment to calibrate, to figure out what she's hearing.

SAM. Rain. Thunder. Violent wind. It sounds big. The news had warned it was coming. Said it would be in for a few days.

SAFIYYA. Within the chaos of this summer storm, though, there's something else. A clanging. A banging.

SAM. Maybe someone's trying to break in, Carly thinks to herself. Maybe someone is breaking in and at this exact moment I'm doing nothing about it. Someone could be knocking down my door with a hammer and a crowbar, and I'm just lying here.

MARCIA. Carly listens to Noah's small, sleepy gurgles. Tries to communicate telepathically with him.

ALL. Please don't wake up please don't wake up please don't wake up please don't wake up

SAFIYYA. She lies there staring into the blackness of the room, considering the painful prospect of leaving her soft cocoon to investigate. But the banging doesn't stop.

SAM. She untangles her sweaty limbs from the covers, raising up the lead weight of her body. She slips her feet into the worn sheepskin slippers discarded by the side of her bed and shrugs on her dressing gown.

MARCIA. In the living room, the banging sounds louder still. The early-onset hangover erupts unforgivingly inside her skull.

SAFIYYA. Is this a dream? A nightmare?

MARCIA. Looking to the balcony door, Carly realises the sound is coming from outside.

She pulls the dressing gown tighter around her

Turns the key in the lock

Pulls open the door

And steps out into the storm.

The thunderstorm grows louder.

SAFIYYA. Harsh winds and driving rain lash Carly's face.

SAM. The air is hot.

SAFIYYA. Thunder rumbles threateningly overhead.

SAM. Lightning flashes across the sky and for a moment it's like Carly can see the whole of London.

MARCIA. Up on tiptoes, she strains to peek over the wall to number sixty-one. The balcony door is open and swinging violently back and forth in the wind. Slamming over and over against the concrete wall behind it.

SAFIYYA. Who could ignore that sound? Nobody. Unless they couldn't hear it. Unless –

SAM. A wave of nausea washes over Carly.

MARCIA. She runs back into her flat, back to her bed –

SAM. Discarding her now soaked dressing gown and slippers.

SAFIYYA. Desperately, she scoops Noah out of his cot and brings him into her bed. Doesn't care about waking him up. Holds him as close as she possibly can.

SAM. Bleary eyed, he puts a tiny hand to her face.

SAFIYYA. Mama?

MARCIA. It's okay, baby. It's okay. We're okay.

SAM. She screws her eyes shut and tries to force herself back into sleep. But sleep will not come.

She picks up her phone.

SAFIYYA (*as* CARLY). Can anyone hear that?

MARCIA. The replies come quickly. Nobody is asleep.

SAM (*as* LINDA). I can hear it

SAFIYYA (*as* ADEEL). We can even hear it from downstairs

MARCIA (*as* REBECCA). Us too

SAM. Two doors down, Linda –

MARCIA. Frantic, sleep-deprived –

SAM. Stares at Clive's framed face –

MARCIA. Looking back at her from the bedside table.

<u>Enough</u>.

SAM (*as* LINDA). I'm calling the police.

Beat.

SAFIYYA. Two hours later.

MARCIA. A commotion draws the grown-ups to the fourth-floor corridor –

SAFIYYA. It's them. Two officers. Banging fists against number sixty-one.

MARCIA. They're shouting –

SAM. OPEN UP!

SAFIYYA. It seems polite knocks haven't worked.

SAM. OPEN UP!

OPEN UP! POLICE!

MARCIA. Nothing. Nobody. The officers look to each other. Something unspoken.

SAFIYYA. Then, one swift, hard kick

And the cold, plain, white wood door

Quickly splinters and cracks under the pressure. The cheaply made hinge breaks. The door slowly swings open.

Beat.

And it only takes a second

For the police to see what they see

And to turn around to the neighbours who stand, slack-jawed, watching, waiting, and scream, yes, scream

SAM. GET INSIDE

   GO BACK INSIDE

MARCIA. GO BACK TO YOUR FLATS

SAM. NOW

SAFIYYA. NOW

MARCIA. GET BACK INSIDE

SAM. NOW

SAFIYYA. And then they know. In that moment, there can be no more pretending.

MARCIA. The inevitable.

Beat.

SAM. They do what they're told. Retreat into Linda's hallway. Listening.

SAFIYYA. But Jaydn –

SAM. Who has woken in his bed to the sounds of shouting on the floor above –

SAFIYYA. And his mother nowhere to be seen –

SAM. Has made his way sleepily up the flight of stairs, pyjama-clad –

SAFIYYA. Exiting the stairwell to find himself directly in front of the open door of number sixty-one –

MARCIA. And he sees.

   He sees he sees he sees he sees he sees what he shouldn't and it cannot be unseen and what he sees is –

   Shirley.

SAFIYYA. Oh. Yeah. Her name was Shirley, by the way.

A moment.

SAM. Shirley is found –

MARCIA. No.

SAFIYYA. Shirley's body is found –

MARCIA. No, that's not right.

SAM. Shirley's remains are found –

MARCIA. No, that's not right either.

SAFIYYA. Shirley's corpse is found –

MARCIA. No, that's not right, it's not right, it's not right –

SAM. What are we meant to say? Jaydn doesn't see a person. He doesn't see Shirley.

SAFIYYA. It's not her any more.

MARCIA. No. I know.

He just sees –

Bones. The bones of a person. The bare bones of a life.

A moment.

SAFIYYA. They couldn't find out what made her...

SAM. Go.

SAFIYYA. Yes. No. They couldn't know what made her go, you know –

SAM. How she

MARCIA. Or why she

SAFIYYA. Or what

MARCIA. Made Shirley... go.

SAM. Unexplained, but not suspicious.

MARCIA. She was too –

I mean, it had been too –

Long.

SAM. A whole year.

SAFIYYA. 376 days, to be exact.

SAM. 9,024 hours.

MARCIA. 32,486,400 seconds.

And Shirley was right there. The whole time.

SAFIYYA. Just next door.

7. The Bit After

SAM. Wednesday. The next day. 6.56 p.m. Linda returns to her flat laden with shopping bags and breathless because today –

SAFIYYA. Today of all days –

MARCIA. The lift is not working.

SAM. Linda half-places, half-drops the bags to the floor. The contents spill out: bleach, disinfectant, sprays, sponges, J-cloths, disposable gloves. Having been working all day –

SAFIYYA. Putting on a normal face –

SAM. Linda changes into old tracksuit bottoms and a saggy, stained T-shirt which have seen better days but are reserved for –

I don't want to say times like these, because there've never been times like these, but – reserved for grubby work.

Linda pulls on a pair of disposable gloves. Then a second pair on top. She retrieves the Marigolds from under the sink and pulls those on, too. She tries to open a packet of sponges.

SAFIYYA. It's difficult, with the gloves.

MARCIA. Sponges fly everywhere. She frantically scoops them up.

SAM. Armed with a bottle of industrial cleaning spray in each hand, Linda douses every surface. Tiles, cabinets, sink. She drizzles bleach over everything. Fills a bucket with steaming hot water and glugs of disinfectant. Mops the floors, the skirting boards, the walls, even. She scrubs desperately.

Fervently. Furiously. The filth is in the walls and she can feel it in her bones and under her skin.

MARCIA. As she works, Linda accidentally knocks the pink, porcelain, pig-shaped biscuit jar gifted to her by Clive. As if in slow motion, it tumbles to the cold, hard, linoleum floor.

SAFIYYA. It breaks.

Beat.

SAM. A sob escapes Linda's throat. Then another. She covers her mouth with her arm, as if to stop the sobs from escaping. But they break free anyway. She cries, hard. But only for a few minutes.

MARCIA. Then Linda pushes it all back down and carries on scrubbing.

...

SAFIYYA. Friday. Two days after. 9.17 p.m.

Adeel and Aleena Bakash lay out two prayer mats onto their living-room carpet, kneel, and pray their maghrib salah. Nothing new to Adeel, who hasn't wavered in his five daily prayers for the entirety of his adult life. Aleena though, has withdrawn for the last two years. Sickness took her mum. What kind of Allah would do that?

Tonight though, instead of going into Soho for her friend's nineteenth, Aleena spends Friday night in the flat with her father and prays.

As they bow their heads in unison, for Aleena it feels at once brand-new, and like she never stopped.

MARCIA. The familiar rhythm

SAM. The softness of the mat against her forehead

SAFIYYA. The quiet, comforting sound of Adeel's breath and soft 'Allahu Akbar, Allahu Akbar' synchronising with her own.

...

SAM. At Carly's –

MARCIA. She can barely stand being at home, being next door to –

She doesn't know what to do.

SAM. So she makes a phone call. One she hasn't made in nearly two years.

Beat.

Mum?

…

MARCIA. Saturday night. Three days after.

Jaydn Abiola –

Who likes to act grown, act tough, act like he knows the world –

He cannot sleep. He cannot sleep at all. He cannot get the image out of his head of the woman at number sixty-one and the way she used to smile at him at the bus stop sometimes and the way she became just bones, just bones, just bones.

On one of these sleepless nights, Jaydn climbs out of his bed and tip-toes down the hall to his mum's room

Stopping for a moment outside her bedroom door, slightly ajar, willing himself to just go back to bed

But he can't,

He softly pushes open the door

Half-enters the room

And whispers into the darkness

SAFIYYA. Mum?

SAM. Mum doesn't stir or move

But Mum is not asleep.

MARCIA. Mum is also in the throes of another restless night.

Another night staring into the darkness

Thinking about all the people she works with at the end of their lives, and how, truthfully, so few of us really make an impact on this world. None of us are going to be remembered. We all want to think we're special but we're not. There was probably a time in Shirley's life when she thought she was going to be special, and Rebecca and Shirley are not so different, really. That wasn't dignity, that wasn't dignity in death, not what she's been taught –

SAFIYYA. Mum?

Beat.

MARCIA. Son? Are you okay?

SAFIYYA. Mum. I can't sleep.

Mum, can I… can I sleep in your bed tonight?

MARCIA. Rebecca doesn't need to say anything. Her baby boy. Her whole heart. She pulls back the duvet and Jaydn climbs in. She holds him close and whispers in his ear and strokes his hair as hot tears fall from his eyes in an unstoppable flood.

It's okay. We're gonna be okay. I promise you, we're gonna be okay.

SAFIYYA. For the first time, Rebecca doesn't feel sure that she's telling her son the truth.

…

SAM. Media people swarm Laurel House, feeding hungrily on the rot of this story.

MARCIA. They knock on doors. Seems to be no trouble for them.

SAM. Linda is caught off guard in her dressing gown. Adeel is cooking dinner.

SAFIYYA. Carly hasn't even got her make-up on.

MARCIA. Rebecca is about to leave for work. She doesn't want to be seen on TV in her ugly uniform.

SAM. They're all quizzed about the woman at number sixty-one.

Shirley, yeah. Her name was Shirley. She seemed like a really nice lady.

MARCIA. My son saw her at the bus stop sometimes.

SAFIYYA. I saw her carrying her shopping sometimes.

SAM. Carly, for some reason, says –

I think I knew her better than anyone, to be honest? We didn't really talk though. Only hello and you alright and all that.

MARCIA. Non-statements of little substance. Things just to say, in the absence of anything tangible. Anything real.

SAFIYYA. It's Adeel that says –

I did not know her. None of us did. But I am praying for her. I am praying for her.

Beat.

MARCIA. Cameras zoom in on Shirley's front door

Splintered wood, muddy boot print still visible

And adorned with a makeshift shrine that the tenants have erected.

SAM. Five scented candles, which Carly has picked out very carefully to fill these corridors with soothing scents. Lavender, freesia, bergamot, eucalyptus, rose.

SAFIYYA. And four bunches of white lilies from Lidl, now wilting.

...

SAM. A couple of weeks later, the housing puts out a statement.

SAFIYYA. A dead-eyed, unmoved man –

SAM. Not Darren, but not unlike Darren. Someone higher up in the pecking order. Reading off a screen.

SAFIYYA. Fatigue –

MARCIA. Boredom, even –

SAFIYYA. Etched across his face.

SAM (*as housing*). We didn't join the dots.

But we did make many attempts –

Eighty-nine attempts, in fact –

To reach out.

But we failed to communicate properly –

And we failed to connect.

MARCIA. Never mind what they were being told. Never mind what was being shouted in their faces.

SAM. We don't know that Shirley was lonely. But we do know that she was very much on her own.

Nevertheless, we didn't do what we were supposed to do, and for that we are deeply, extremely, personally, unabashedly, shamefully, remorsefully, painfully, unequivocally, terribly, awfully, sorry.

Sorry if the situation caused any… inconvenience. Sorry if you felt upset.

The crux of it, however, is that yes we should have realised, and yes, we should have done more. That much is true. Of course.

SAFIYYA. Of course.

SAM. But the fact of the matter is –

She was already dead.

So. Nothing we could've done there. Nothing we could've done to stop that. We couldn't have saved her life.

SAFIYYA. She was already dead.

MARCIA. She was already dead.

A moment.

As the reporters dissipate from Laurel House, Linda overhears one say –

SAM. They say she had a four-pack of crème caramels left in her fridge. How sad is that? Sadder than anything. What a waste. Can't think of anything sadder than an uneaten dessert.

8. The Day of Shirley's Death

MARCIA. The day of Shirley's death was mundane, which is to say, it was the same as every other day.

SAFIYYA. No better, no worse. Nothing out of the ordinary.

SAM. On the day of her death, Shirley woke up and took a shower, feeling irritated when the water ran cold halfway through. Again.

SAFIYYA. Shirley ate a bowl of bran flakes, which were stale, because she forgot to fold the bag over the last time she ate the bran flakes.

SAM. Shirley missed a call from her doctor, and didn't find time to phone them back.

MARCIA. On the Tube, Shirley was offered a seat by a young person, which was intended as a kind gesture but which offended Shirley, because she was only fifty-eight, and what had the years done to weather her face and body so prematurely?

SAFIYYA. Shirley stroked the ears of a stranger's golden retriever and wondered whether it would be good for her to get a pet.

SAM. Shirley was shouted at by someone at work who she was only trying to help.

MARCIA. Shirley considered the fact that her life hadn't turned out the way she thought it would, but she couldn't really remember how she wanted it to turn out in the first place, so maybe it didn't really matter.

SAFIYYA. Shirley bought a shopping basket of impractical groceries that nobody could make a meal with: a bunch of bananas, a multipack of Walker's crisps in assorted flavours, and a four-pack of crème caramel desserts.

SAM. Shirley said hello to three people in her block. They said hello back, and nothing more.

MARCIA. Shirley climbed the four flights of stairs to her flat to exercise her legs, which were giving her trouble again. She regretted this decision about one floor up, but wanted to save face for herself, so carried on.

SAFIYYA. Shirley ate crisps for dinner: ready salted.

SAM. Shirley gave herself permission to have a little nightcap of sherry, which she drank whilst laying on the sofa.

SAFIYYA. Shirley considered eating one of the crème caramels. She'd earned it, she thought, for climbing the stairs. But the fridge felt so far away.

SAM. Instead, Shirley poured herself a second glass of sherry.

SAFIYYA. In a fuzzy sherry stupor, a thought flashed into Shirley's mind: how long had it been since she'd been held in the arms of another?

MARCIA. As this thought dissolved, Shirley fell asleep right there on the sofa, and the next morning, Shirley didn't wake up.

A moment.

SAM. That's all made up, though.

MARCIA. We don't know any of that.

SAFIYYA. These are just the gaps you have to fill in.

MARCIA. The unknown crevices. The dark, blank spaces.

SAM. The dusty corners of a life.

> Shirley. A person seemingly without a past, and now without a future.

SAFIYYA. No friends –

> No family –
>
> No discernible interests or hobbies.

MARCIA. No digital footprint, somehow – except for a single Facebook post ten years prior, in which she searches for a friend from school:

```
I am looking for Audrey Douglas who I
went to school with I can't remember
your address and made the mistake of not
writing it down
```

SAM. And a three-by-three centimetre passport photograph that does the rounds on the news. Shirley, in faded colours. Unsmiling. Blank.

MARCIA. Giving absolutely nothing away.

9. The End

SAM. The revelation of Shirley's death brings about a series of radical shifts.

SAFIYYA. Once the dust has settled, Linda opens the Laurel House tenants' group chat once more.

MARCIA (*as* LINDA). ```Coffee mornings, once a week at mine?```

SAM. People come! And they get to know each other. Adeel brings his famous homemade cumin cookies. Carly comes along with Noah. Everyone takes turns holding him, agreeing that it's impossible to be sad while cuddling a bundle of joy with chubby little arm rolls.

MARCIA. In August, Jaydn passes his GCSEs with top marks! Next stop, A level physics.

SAFIYYA. Come September, Aleena swans off to Cambridge. In his daughter's absence, Adeel starts a community initiative to get neighbours talking to each other. He calls it 'Knock knock, I'm here'. Aleena posts about it on TikTok, and before he knows it, his little idea has gone national. Adeel, on the news! Making a difference.

MARCIA. Rebecca's late-night trysts with Darnell evolve into something more meaningful. She feels loved –

SAFIYYA. Seen –

MARCIA. For the first time in forever.

SAM. Carly reconnects with her parents. Her mum moves in for a while, to help out.

MARCIA. And the neighbours, too – enamoured as they are with Noah – agree to chip in with babysitting, when they can.

SAM. With her load eased, Carly enrols on a social-work course. Something just for her.

MARCIA. The housing is held accountable. Heads roll. Darren is fired. New protocols are put in place.

SAFIYYA. The housing organises a funeral for Shirley. Hundreds attend. Her life is finally seen, finally known.

MARCIA. Her death meant something. Her death changed something.

A long moment. The STORYTELLERS *bask in this happy ending and allow the audience to do the same. Eventually –*

SAM. Be nice, wouldn't it? All of that.

SAFIYYA. It's not quite what happens, though.

Linda *does* suggest coffee mornings, and they *do* happen –

SAM. For a bit.

SAFIYYA. Three, maybe four times. Then everyone gets a bit busy.

MARCIA. On GCSE results day, Jaydn discovers he has failed nearly everything.

SAM. Turns out, trying to revise next door to a rotting corpse isn't conducive to academic success.

MARCIA. But he'll re-take. Rebecca will make sure of that.

SAFIYYA. Aleena does go off to Cambridge. She's racked with guilt about leaving her dad at a time like this – but she's got to go. Got to get away from Laurel House.

SAM. Jaydn, scrolling Aleena's Instagram longingly, is stopped in his tracks by her most recent post – smiling ear to ear, with her arm around her new Cambridge girlfriend.

SAFIYYA. Ohhhhh. Oh, right.

MARCIA. With Aleena gone, Adeel's heart is once again torn apart by grief. But this time, partially healed by pride.

SAM. He does take some solace in a newfound, tentative friendship with Linda –

SAFIYYA. No, not like *that*.

But the crockery dish of warm biryani that he delivers to Linda's front door is unlike anything that has passed her lips before. Even –

SAM. Dare she say it –

SAFIYYA. Clive's Christmas veg.

MARCIA. Carly's mum doesn't move in. But she does start visiting. Sometimes –

SAM. Often –

MARCIA. They argue. Carly can't just forgive and forget. But she's still glad to have her around.

Passing Carly's mum in the corridor one day, Rebecca learns why she's been doing this alone.

Her stomach fills with white-hot rage.

SAM. So Rebecca knocks on Carly's door and offers to help with Noah, sometimes.

SAFIYYA. She doesn't have the time or energy –

MARCIA. But she knows it takes a village.

Rebecca can't move past what this did to *her* baby. What he saw.

SAM. Darnell decides he can't hack it – didn't sign up for all this heavy emotional shit.

SAFIYYA. Jaydn can't take the night terrors. The memories.

MARCIA. She tries to move them out. But getting rehoused is not easy. And this is –

SAFIYYA. Or should be –

MARCIA. Their home.

Beat.

SAM. Darren.

Darren quits his job.

Not because he suddenly understands the full weight of what went wrong.

Not because he's woken up to his own failures, and the failures of the systems that are meant to look after us.

SAFIYYA. No. He quits simply because he is very very very very very very scared that something like this might happen again.

MARCIA. There is an inquiry of sorts. Half-arsed. But nobody is held accountable –

SAM. Obviously.

SAFIYYA. So that's… kind of it.

(*Excited.*) Oh! One important thing does happen.

SAM. Linda –

MARCIA. Finding herself gripped by a newfound, furious hunger for life –

SAM. Books flights to see her daughter Josie, 10,573 miles away in Sydney, Australia.

MARCIA. She cannot afford it.

SAFIYYA. She does not care.

SAM. So no radical changes.

MARCIA. A few small shifts.

SAFIYYA. The fabric of the Laurel House community –

SAM. Subtly –

MARCIA. Imperfectly –

SAFIYYA. Rewoven.

MARCIA. Just a small residential block on a quiet street, off a busy road, in an unremarkable corner of London.

A shared breath. The STORYTELLERS *shed the story. They look to the audience. Perhaps a small nod. An acknowledgement.*

Then, quietly, they leave.

End of play.

A Nick Hern Book

Maggots first published in Great Britain in 2026 as a paperback original by Nick Hern Books Limited, The Glasshouse, 49a Goldhawk Road, London W12 8QP in association with the Bush Theatre, London, and Jessie Anand Productions

Maggots copyright © 2026 Farah Najib

Farah Najib has asserted her moral right to be identified as the author of this work

Cover image: Harry Elletson

Designed and typeset by Nick Hern Books, London
Printed in the UK by Mimeo Ltd, Huntingdon, Cambridgeshire PE29 6XX

A CIP catalogue record for this book is available from the British Library

ISBN 978 1 83904 542 4

CAUTION All rights whatsoever in this play are strictly reserved. Requests to reproduce the text in whole or in part should be addressed to the publisher. This book may not be used, in whole or in part, for the development or training of artificial intelligence technologies or systems.

Amateur Performing Rights Applications for performance, including readings and excerpts, by amateurs in the English language throughout the world should be addressed to the Performing Rights Department, Nick Hern Books, The Glasshouse, 49a Goldhawk Road, London W12 8QP, *tel* +44 (0)20 8749 4953, *email* rights@nickhernbooks.co.uk, except as follows:

Australia: ORiGiN Theatrical, Level 1, 213 Clarence Street, Sydney NSW 2000, *tel* +61 (2) 8514 5201, *email* enquiries@originmusic.com.au, *web* www.origintheatrical.com.au

New Zealand: Play Bureau, 20 Rua Street, Mangapapa, Gisborne, 4010, *tel* +64 21 258 3998, *email* info@playbureau.com

United States and Canada: United Agents, see details below

Professional Performing Rights Applications for performance by professionals in any medium and in any language throughout the world (including by stock companies in the USA and Canada) should be addressed to United Agents Ltd, 12–26 Lexington St, London W1F 0LE, tel +44 (0)20 3214 0800, fax +44 (0)20 3214 0801, email info@unitedagents.co.uk

No performance of any kind may be given unless a licence has been obtained. Applications should be made before rehearsals begin. Publication of this play does not necessarily indicate its availability for amateur performance.

www.nickhernbooks.co.uk/environmental-policy

Nick Hern Books' authorised representative in the EU is
Easy Access System Europe – Mustamäe tee 50, 10621 Tallinn, Estonia
email gpsr.requests@easproject.com